The New Ibis Readers Book Three

by Olly N. Stanford
and Esmee E. Mejias

Illustrated by Lisa Kopper

AN HACHETTE UK COMPANY

Note to the teacher

Book Three is the last of the Infant Readers. This new edition has the same text as previously but it has been repaged to make 48 pages instead of 64 pages. The text of the earlier readers will have given pupils a vocabulary of at least 237 words. However the pupils will have learned to read many more words from other books, classroom activities, labels, word-building exercises, etc. They should also have developed a certain measure of confidence in their ability to read and an eagerness to begin to explore the fascinating world of books.

This reader contains 256 new words in addition to the 237 of the previous readers. These words are listed on Pages 45–6. Lessons are arranged in units and there are "Read and Do" exercises at the end of each unit.

Simple instructions are provided in italics. Some of these words will not have been used in the Reading Scheme. The teacher should read these aloud to pupils until they begin to recognize the words and can read them for themselves. In the exercises the missing word *only* should be written. This should be done in the pupil's own Note Book and *not* in the textbook.

The stories are now continuous so that pupils can acquire fluency in reading. Some puzzles have been included on Page 44. These challenge the children's powers of observation and are useful aids in beginning oral composition.

The lessons are based on subjects which will be familiar to pupils as well as providing imaginative stories and poems. Topics chosen in this book will help prepare pupils for the additional subjects of the Junior School curriculum, such as, Social Studies, Science, Art, Language and Literature.

Poetry

Two simple poems, *The Wind* and *Carnival* form part of the text. However, the poem *A West Indian Year Song* on Page 43 does not. This poem is intended to be read by the teacher and the children encouraged to learn it. In addition, other suitable poems should often be read aloud so that the children can enjoy the music of words and develop an interest in poetry.

The phonics programme

This is a natural follow-on from work done in *Books One* and *Two*. The name and sound of each letter of the alphabet as well as the short and long vowel sounds must be revised. New consonant digraphs and blends should be introduced and the old ones revised.

In this Reader the following skills are dealt with:—

1. Vowel combinations: *ai, ea, oa, oi, ou, ee* and *oo*.
2. Final vowel and consonant combinations: *ay, oy, ow, er, ir, ur* and *or*.
3. Change in number forms – singular and plural.
4. Change in tense – present and past.
5. The past participle and the addition of *ing*.
6. Words that sound alike.

The teacher should use words from the text and other examples to provide practice in the skills for the pupils. Some examples are given on pages 47 and 48, together with some very useful vocabulary.

With this phonics programme the use of the pupil's own Word Book, as well as the Practice Book for this Reader cannot be too strongly emphasized.

The classroom

The Teacher's Notes for *Book Two* introduced some ideas for arranging centres of interest in the classroom. The teacher should try to develop these areas over the year.

The books in the Book Corner must be changed now to keep pace with the pupils' increased ability to read. There should be wall pockets or other similar receptacles containing instructions for work for the pupils to do, for example, in reading, in number work, and in creative activities. This work should be carefully graded and labelled so that the pupils can move easily, step by step, through the relevant activity.

Instruction notices like these will help the pupils to carry out the daily programme:-

1. Work sums on your card.
2. Read at the Book Corner.
3. Put new words in your Word Book.

Making books for the Book Corner is another very useful activity at this stage. Pupils can write their own little stories, for example, "All About Me", "My Pet", "Things I Like to Do". They may then be helped to fold, sew or staple the pages together to make little books. Designs on the covers can also be done by the pupils.

Orders: please contact Hachette UK Distribution, Hely Hutchinson Centre, Milton Road, Didcot, Oxfordshire, OX11 7HH. Telephone: +44 (0)1235 827827. Email education@hachette.co.uk Lines are open from 9 a.m. to 5 p.m., Monday to Friday. You can also order through our website: www.hoddereducation.com

© Olly N. Stanford and Esmee E. Mejias 1985

All rights reserved. Apart from any use permitted under UK copyright law, no part of this publication may be reproduced or transmitted in any form or by any means, electronic or mechanical, including photocopying and recording, or held within any information storage and retrieval system, without permission in writing from the publisher or under licence from the Copyright Licensing Agency Limited. Further details of such licences (for reprographic reproduction) may be obtained from the Copyright Licensing Agency Limited, www.cla.co.uk.

First published by Collins Educational 1985
First published by Longman Group UK Ltd 1988
Published from 2015 by Hodder Education,
An Hachette UK Company
Carmelite House
50 Victoria Embankment
London EC4Y 0DZ
www.hoddereducation.com

Seventeenth impression 2017

25
IMP 7

Printed in Great Britain by Ashford Colour Press Ltd.

ISBN 978-0-582-03453-2

The coconut

Here is a coconut cart. There are many coconuts on this cart. I like green coconuts. There is water in a green coconut. When we cut a green coconut we can get the water to drink. We can get soft, white jelly too.

There are many cars by this cart. We can see Peter and Carol in one of these cars. They want to get some coconut water to drink. They want some jelly too. They like to eat the soft, white jelly.

The man by the cart is cutting the coconuts quickly. Chop! Chop! Chop! Chop! He has to cut many of them. When he has cut the coconuts he puts the shells on his cart.

Daddy, Mummy, Peter and Carol are going for a drive. They are going to the beach. David is with them. Can you see the coconut trees on each side of the road? Coconut trees are tall trees. How big the leaves are! The leaves and the fruit are at the top of the tree.

Peter has a bat that is made from a coconut leaf. He and David like to play with this bat.

Here are some dry coconuts. "What are the men doing with these dry coconuts?" asks Peter.

"Let us stop and see," says Daddy. He stops the car and they get out.

They see how the men cut open the dry coconuts. The soft, white jelly is now hard. What will the men do with it?

What the wind can do

The wind blows. It blows the leaves from the trees. It blows the kites up high. It blows the shirts on the line. It blows my hat away.

    We can hear the wind when it blows. We can feel it too. We say that we can feel the breeze. We like to feel the breeze.

    Can we see the wind? No, we cannot see the wind but we can see the trees bend when the wind blows.

    What is wind?

The wind

See the trees bend
An ear to lend
To the splash of the waves.

Hear the waves splash
And splash and splash
Upon the sandy beach.

See the birds fly
Up high in the sky,
They like the clean fresh breeze.

Hear the wind blow,
Where will it go?
I cannot say, can you?

Read and do

*Read the stories and poem again.
Then answer the questions.
Write the words in your Note Book.*

The coconut

1. We can drink the . . . from the green coconuts.
2. We get soft, . . ., . . ., from green coconuts too.
3. Coconut trees are . . . trees.
4. Peter made his bat from a . . ., ...
5. The men cut open . . . (the dry coconuts/the coconut leaves/Peter's bat.)

What the wind can do

1. We can . . . the wind but we cannot . . . it.
2. The wind . . . the kites up high.
3. The trees . . . (bend/stand/blow) in the wind.

The wind

1. The waves . . . on the beach.
2. The birds like the . . . breeze.

Things to do

What is at the top of the coconut tree?
Draw some coconut trees.

Looking at things

Joy likes flowers. She likes red roses. She goes in to the garden to water her roses. She takes a broom to brush away the dry leaves.

What is she looking at? She is looking at a spider. The spider is spinning a web. How quickly it spins!

Some spiders are big and some are little. This is a little spider. How many legs has a spider? Can you see the legs on this one? How many are there? There are one, two, three, four, five, six, seven, eight legs.

Now the spider sits in the web. Joy looks at it. What is it doing now? Soon she will see.

A fly comes by. It is a big fly. The spider moves very quickly. It catches the fly. Now Joy sees why the spider made a web. The fly is the spider's lunch.

Joy is in the garden again today. This time she has a little bottle in her hand. She is looking for a caterpillar. She wants to take the caterpillar to school. She wants it for the nature table.

Here is a green caterpillar. It is on a leaf. It is eating the leaf. It is eating very quickly. Joy puts the caterpillar in her bottle. She is glad. She has a caterpillar to take to school. She will put some holes in the cover of the bottle so that the caterpillar can get air.

The caterpillar is now on the nature table. Each day Joy has to feed it with leaves. A caterpillar eats and grows. It grows and eats. Soon it will eat no more. It will spin a little home for itself. It will not move in this little home for some time.

The children look at it each day. One day it moves! The children look and look. The teacher comes and looks too. Something is coming out of the little home. What is it? It is a pretty yellow butterfly.

Indra is looking at a book. Her father gave it to her for her birthday. The book is about animals and birds. In the book, Indra can see a lion, a tiger, a cat, a dog and many other animals. She can see a nest with eggs and a bird that looks like a Keskidee. She can see another bird.

"What a pretty bird!" says Indra to herself. "I like this one." She goes to her father. "Look at this pretty bird, father. What bird is it?"

Her father is glad to tell her about the bird. "It is the Scarlet Ibis," he says. "It likes to live near water. See how long its legs are. The long legs help it to walk in the water."

"What a long bill it has!" says Indra.

"Yes," says her father. "The Ibis eats fish and other things it gets from the water. The long bill helps it to find the food it likes."

Do you like your book? What is the name of it? You can see the name on the cover. Can you read it? Yes, you can. The name is *The New Ibis Readers*.

What more do you see on the cover? Yes, you can see many birds. What birds are they? Can you tell? What are they doing? Your teacher will tell you much more about these birds.

Read and do

*Read the story again.
Then answer the questions.
Write the words in your Note Book.*

1. Joy likes . . . .
2. The spider . . . a web . . . .
3. A caterpillar . . . and grows.
4. What did the spider have for lunch?
5. Joy will put the caterpillar on the . . . table.
6. The children see a pretty . . . butterfly.
7. Indra gets a . . . (book/toy/doll) for her birthday.
8. The Ibis has . . . legs.
9. The Ibis likes to live . . . .
10. What is the name of your book?

Things to do

1. Draw a spider's web.
2. Find out how many legs a spider has.
   Draw a spider.

Helping mother

Richard and his little sister live with their father and mother. Their father goes to work each day. He has to go to work early. Richard has to get up early too. He gets out of bed. He helps his mother before he gets ready for school.

No pipes bring water to Richard's home. There is a standpipe up the road. Richard's mother gets water from this pipe. Richard helps his mother to get water.

Today Richard's little sister wants to help. She wants to get water, too. She takes a little pan. She goes up the road with Richard. They have to walk up a little hill to get to the standpipe. They run and skip as they go. Who will get to the standpipe first?

Richard gets there first and fills his pan with water. His sister fills her pan, too.

Now they are coming down the hill. They are going home. They walk with care down the hill. But Richard trips over a stone. He falls. The water from the pan splashes over him.

Before he can get up his sister trips and falls, too. Both children are very wet. There is not a drop of water in their pans.

This is what the standpipe saw.

The nurse

Richard could not go to school today. He had a cut on his head and on his arm. He got the cuts when he fell.

His mother washed the cuts. She put him to bed. Nurse Brown, who lives near, came to see Richard's mother. Richard's mother asked the nurse to look at the cuts on Richard's head and arm.

Nurse Brown looked at the cuts. She helped Richard's mother to dress them.

She washed them again with clean water. She put something from her bag on them. Then she put a strip of plaster on each cut. Richard could not go out to play with his friend that day.

The nurse came another day to look at Richard's cuts. Richard's head and arm will soon be well again.

A nurse is very kind. She helps us to get well.

The postman

Richard can go to school today. As he came out of the gate he saw the postman. The postman is his friend. Every day he meets this postman. The postman always stops to talk to Richard.

The postman has a bag. Richard knows that the bag has letters in it because the postman is doing his work. Today the postman has a letter in his hand. It is for Richard's mother. He gives the letter to Richard. Richard takes it and looks at it. He likes to look at the stamps on letters.

At school the teacher has told the children about stamps. They keep a stamp book. Richard runs back to the house quickly and gives the letter to his mother. His mother gives him the stamp. Richard is glad to have it. He will take it to school.

Read and do

*Read the stories again.
Answer the questions.
Write the answers in your Note Book.*

Helping mother

1. The standpipe was . . . .
2. Richard helps his mother to get . . . .
3. Who got to the standpipe first?
4. Richard . . . over a stone.
5. What did the standpipe see?

The nurse

1. Richard got a . . . when he fell.
2. The nurse put a . . . of . . . . on Richard's cut.
3. Who helps us to get well?

The postman

1. What did the postman have in his bag?
2. The postman gives the . . . to Richard.
3. What did the children keep at school?
4. What did Richard take to school?

The rainbow

David stood at the window looking out at the rain. The rain had been falling for a long time. Was it never going to stop? How much longer was it going to fall?

David wanted to go over to Peter's house. Peter had got a new toy from the store. It was a present from his father. He had told David about it and had asked him to come over and see it. David's mother told him that he could go over to Peter's house when the rain stopped.

David pressed his nose against the window pane. Was the rain never going to stop? Was he never going over to Peter's house? He took up a story book and sat down to read.

Soon he put the book down and looked out of the window again. It looked as if the rain was going to stop. The sun was coming out. The sky was getting blue. David saw a beautiful rainbow in the sky. It went from one side of the sky right over to the other side. He could not see the end of it. He stood at the window and looked and looked.

His mother saw the rainbow, too. She came to the window and stood by David.

"Look, mother," said David. "What a beautiful rainbow!"

"Yes," said his mother, "it is a very beautiful rainbow."

"What makes a rainbow?" asked David.

"I remember reading a story about a rainbow," said his mother. "I will tell you about it."

Here is the story David's mother told him.

The rainbow story

One day two little clouds were playing in the sky. They were having fun. In their play they bumped their heads. They bumped them hard. They began to cry. They cried for a long time.

Father Sun came from behind a big cloud. He saw the two little clouds crying.

"Come now, my children," he said. "It is time to stop crying. You have been crying too long. Dry your tears. I will ask some of my little friends to help you dry them."

Very soon the little friends came. There were seven of them. They had on beautiful dresses and each dress was a different colour. The colours were violet, indigo, blue, green, yellow, orange and red.

The seven friends helped the little clouds to dry their tears. They dried the tears with their dresses. The dresses got very wet.

They put them out to dry on a long line Father Sun had made. The dresses looked beautiful on the line. When Father Sun was shining on them, the colours of the dresses made a rainbow.

David liked the story very much. He looked out of the window.

"Look, mother," he said. "The rainbow is still there. I can see the beautiful colours. Will you tell me the names again?"

"Yes," said his mother, "I will tell you. The names are violet, indigo, blue, green, yellow, orange and red."

By this time the rain had stopped and David went over to Peter's house to see his new toy. He told him the story of the two clouds.

"Come and see the beautiful rainbow," he said.

David and Peter went out but the rainbow was not there.

"The dresses must be dry now," said Peter.

"Yes," said David. "The rain has stopped and the sun is shining."

Read and do

*Read the story again.
Answer the questions.
Write the answers in your Note Books.*

1. Peter got a . . . from his father.
2. David . . . his . . . against the window . . . .
3. David saw a beautiful . . . in the sky.
4. Who saw the rainbow?
5. His mother . . . him a . . . about a rainbow.
6. Give another name for the clouds' tears.
7. Who came from behind a big cloud?
8. The rainbow has . . . colours.
9. Who helped the little clouds to dry their tears?
10. What did David do when the rain stopped?

Things to do

1. Write the names of the colours of the rainbow.
2. Draw a rainbow.

Making masks

At school the children like to draw. They always have fun when they draw. Today the teacher, Miss Rose, let them draw faces. The children drew funny faces. While the children drew, Miss Rose walked around the class. She looked at the work of each child.

She told the children that they could colour the faces. The children were glad. They like to colour what they draw.

"Now," said the teacher, "you can cut out the faces. Take your time and do it well. We are going to make some masks with the faces."

At the end of the lesson, Miss Rose put the masks up so that all the children could see them.

One mask had a long nose and a big mouth, another mask had very big ears, a third mask had a red face and blue eyes. They were all very funny. The children laughed at all the funny faces. The teacher laughed too.

"What funny masks you have made," she said. "Let us have a party soon."

A carnival party

The children are very happy. This is Friday, the day of the party. It is a Carnival party. Each child has on a funny mask. They made these masks in school a few days before.

Here is one of them with a long nose and a big mouth. Do you know who it is? It is David. He is making everyone laugh with his funny face. Here are Joy and Carol. Joy has on the mask with the big ears. Carol has on a pretty costume. Where is Indra? Can you see her? She is the only one with a tall hat.

The children are jumping to the music of the steel band. Steel band music makes you want to jump. Some big boys are playing the steel band music.

Two small boys are standing by the band. They are looking at the big boys as they play. The small boys are in costume. One of them is Peter. Can you tell which? Yes, he has on the mask with the red face and blue eyes.

Carnival

I hear music,
Loud music, sweet music,
The steel band is playing,
Masqueraders are jumping.

I see costumes,
Pretty costumes, gay costumes,
There are many colours,
I want to paint them all.

I am happy,
Very, very happy,
It is Carnival time,
Let's all join in the fun.

Read and do

*Read the stories and poem again.
Answer the questions.
Write the answers in your Note Book.*

Making masks

1. The children made . . . for the party.
2. They like to . . . what they draw.
3. Why did the teacher laugh?

A carnival party

1. Who has on the mask with the long nose and big mouth?
2. Who has on the mask with the big ears?
3. Indra had on a . . . .
4. The music made the children . . . .
5. Big boys play . . . on the steel . . . .
6. This is a . . . (birthday/carnival/dolls') party.

Carnival

1. The music was . . . and sweet.

Things to do

Draw a funny mask, colour it and cut it out.

A class outing

It is a sunny morning. There is a bus at the school gate. Inside the school some children are getting ready to go on an outing with their teacher.

They soon come out and get into the bus. The bus moves off. Where are they going? Let us go with them and we shall see.

At first the bus goes by the Zoo and then along the highway. The teacher points out different places as they go along. They see a milk factory, a bottle factory, a big supermarket and a jam factory. They see many children who want to cross the road. A policeman stops the cars on both sides of the road and the children cross quickly.

The children in the bus hear a loud noise. They look out and see a plane flying overhead. It is going to the airport.

The bus turns off the highway and follows a long, narrow road. This road takes them to a big house. It is like a seaside house. There they see an old woman.

This old woman looks after the house. The old woman knows the teacher. The children leave their lunch at this house. They get some coconut water to drink.

After a while they set out. They are going for a nature walk. The children laugh and talk as they go. Soon they come to a river. They cross over the river on a little bridge.

"Look!" says one of the boys. "I can see some little fish in the water." The children stop to look. They can see little fish darting here and darting there in the water.

As they get to the other side of the river they hear, "Croak! Croak!" and a big frog hops on to a large stone. Some of the children hurry away. They do not like frogs.

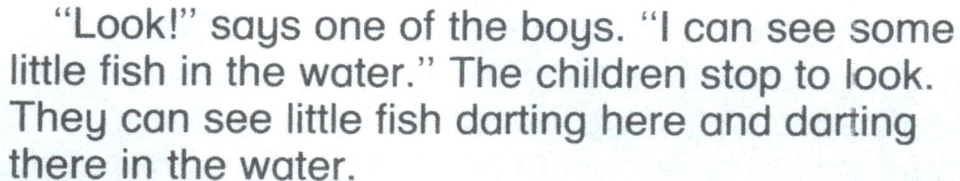

"There is a bird!" cries one of the girls. "What pretty blue feathers it has!" The children keep very quiet and look to see where the bird is going. It flies to a tree. There could be a nest in that tree. The nest could have some baby birds in it. The bird flies around again. "Tweet! Tweet!" it says and flies away.

"See what we have found!" call out two of the boys. The children all rush to see.

"What is it?" they ask.

"It is a grasshopper," says the teacher. "See how long its legs are!" The grasshopper gives a big hop and hops away.

Just then a butterfly comes by. Another follows. The children try to catch one but it flies away. The children see many things. They take back some of these things for the nature table. One child has some wild flowers. Another has different leaves. A third has got a strange fruit.

"We will take it to school and see if we can find out the name," says the teacher.

Soon it is time to go back. At the big house the children have their lunch. The old woman is very kind. She takes them to see the hens and chicks. They see rabbits too. These rabbits have brown spots just like Aunt Jane's rabbits. A little pet kitten follows the old woman everywhere.

The old woman brings a big box for the teacher. In it is some fruit for the children. There are bananas, mangoes and oranges. The children thank her. They say goodbye and get into the bus.

Soon they are at school once more. They will remember this outing for a long time.

Read and do

*Read the story again.
Answer the questions.
Write the answers in your Note Book.*

1. The bus goes by the . . . and then along the . . . .
2. Where was the plane going?
3. What did the children get to drink?
4. What work did the old woman do?
5. How did the children cross the river?
6. Name three things the children saw while on the nature walk.
7. What did the big frog say?
8. Give a name for a bird's home.
9. Why did the children take the strange fruit to school?
10. What was in the box which the old woman gave to the teacher?

Things to do

Do you like frogs?
Draw a grasshopper or a frog.

Peter's dream

As Peter got into bed one night he looked through his open window. The full moon was very bright. The light came right into his room.

Peter looked at the moon. What a big round thing it was! He remembered something that he had heard in school that day.

"The moon has a face like the clock in the hall."

It was true. The moon and the clock both had big round faces.

Soon Peter fell asleep. Then the moon seemed to come near him. He could see the "Man in the Moon". The Moon Man let down a beam of moonlight through the window on to Peter's bed. Peter put out his hand. He could feel that he was being carried through the window. He seemed to float in the air.

He looked around him. A friendly star twinkled at him. It seemed to say, "Come, play with me." Peter remembered now his mother used to sing for him.

"Twinkle, twinkle little star."

Then he saw what looked like smoke. Two little clouds came by. They were talking to each other.

"I saw the cow," one said. "I saw the cow jump over the moon."

"Dear me!" said the other. "How is it ever going to get down again!"

Then Peter saw a strange, old man sitting on a star. This old man had on a tall hat. He was trying to hit the top of his hat with some small stones.

"Please help me," he called to Peter. "Please hit my hat. If someone hits my hat I can get off this star."

Peter did not stop. The beam of moonlight carried him on. Soon he was on the moon. He thought he saw his dog, Rags. Rags was laughing. Peter got off the beam of light. At once he went up into the air like a ball. Every time he moved he began to bounce like a ball.

He bounced near a fisherman who had a big fish in a small tin.

"My word! My word!" he was saying. "I must get this fish to the shop while it is fresh. Fresh fish is cheap today."

Soon Peter saw a big hole before him. "Now," he thought, "I must not fall into this hole." He did not fall into it. He bounced right over it into a large garden.

He looked around. There were flowers of all kinds. They all had happy faces. They were nodding their heads and talking to one another. He heard a zinnia say to a violet, "Our Queen will soon be here. She is having a rainbow party. The party is for her Aunt May. Her Aunt May has come from Disneyland for the party."

Peter hid himself behind a large stone at one end of the garden. Then he saw the queen herself. Her dress was the colour of indigo. She looked like a beautiful doll. She sat in a small boat which was pulled by six little men who were dressed in red and green. Behind her boat came another. Aunt May was in this one. She was pulled by six little monkeys. They were dressed in blue and yellow.

Last of all came a little man with a big head. He made Peter think of Humpty Dumpty. This little man saw Peter.

"Come out, Peter. Come and join us," he called.

Peter came out. Everyone was glad to see him. They made a large ring and he joined in the fun.

There were many things to eat at this party. There were coconut drops, banana jam and orange drinks. There were snow cones, too, with milk on them. Peter had a happy time.

Soon the party came to an end. Peter looked around for his moonbeam. It was time to go home. He did not see the moonbeam. Had he lost it? Then the moonbeam came out from behind a cloud. Sitting on it was Rags. He had a large bone. Peter was just going to hop on the beam when someone gave him a push. He fell out of the garden. He fell down, down, down.

Just when he thought that he was never going to stop, he heard someone calling his name.

"Peter, Peter, get up or you will be late for school."

Peter opened his eyes. It was his mother.

Read and do

*Read the story again.
Answer the questions.
Write the answers in your Note Book.*

1. How did Peter get to the moon?
2. What did the star say when it twinkled at Peter?
3. What did the little cloud see?
4. What was the old man sitting on a star trying to do?
5. What did the fisherman have in the tin?
6. What did the zinnia say to the violet?
7. Where did Aunt May come from?
8. Why did she come?
9. The little man with the big head made Peter think of someone. Who was it?
10. Why did Peter think he had lost the moonbeam?
11. How did Peter get back home?
12. How do you know that Peter had a dream?

A West Indian year song

January
See how the waving corn-tops sweet
Do bend, the bright New Year to greet!

February
The swish of the scythe rends the February air,
And silver-topped cane-fields are left lying bare.

March
Row upon row of brown earth will hide
Brown seeds of cotton o'er many a hillside.

April
The hill-tops their bonnets of yellow display,
Rustling brown leaves now carpet the way.

May
"Drink!" says the earth in a tender refrain,
All nature seems glad at the sound of the rain.

June
June and the rose wait hand in hand,
To greet the brides o'er all the land.

July
The showers have gladden'd the meadowy way,
Let's join the butterflies dance and play.

August
This is the time for frolic and fun,
Our holiday month has now begun.

September
Watch well the wind till September's done,
The hurricane yet its course may run.

October
Juicy fruit on bunches high,
Tempt the children passing by.

November
Bring in the Harvest! Storms are o'er!
Heav'n hath fill'd our garner floor!

December
The breezes know; they softly blow
And whisper "Peace at Christmas".

OLGA COMMA MAYNARD from *Carib Echoes*

Puzzles

I have long ears,
I can hop very fast.
I nibble my food.
What am I?

I need the wind.
I need a tail.
Run, while I fly,
High up in the sky.
What am I?

I am very hard,
But dogs like me.
I am good for their teeth.
They can put me in a hole.
What am I?

I live in the water.
I can dart here,
I can dart there,
And if you can catch me
You can eat me for lunch.
What am I?

I make the trees bend.
I make the fresh breeze.
You cannot see me,
But you can feel me.
What am I?

Bump me,
Bounce me,
Bat me boys,
I'll not cry or make a noise.
What am I?

I spin a web
To catch my food.
I have eight legs.
What am I?

I come from the sky.
I keep the gardens green and fresh,
I make the trees glad.
But I can make you very wet.
What am I?

Word list

The list contains the 256 new words used in this book. Derivatives are not listed. The numbers refer to the pages on which the words first appear.

p.4 coconut
cart
green
when
cut
soft
white
jelly
p.5 quickly
chop
p.6 side
road
tall
leaves
top
made
leaf
men
open
hard
p.7 wind
high
hat
hear
feel
breeze
bend

p.8 ear
lend
waves
sandy
sky
p.10 red
roses
garden
spider
spinning
web
legs
six
seven
eight
moves
why
p.11 again
bottle
hand
caterpillar
cover
air
p.12 nature
grows

more
itself
teacher
butterfly
father
gave
about
Keskidee
p.13 tell
Scarlet
Ibis
live
near
long
other
bill
food
New
name
Readers
p.15 Richard
sister
their
early
before
pipes
pan
hill
who
p.16 fills
trips
over
stone
falls
saw

p.17 could
had
head
arm
fell
nurse
came
strip
plaster
kind
be
well
p.18 gate
postman
every
always
talk
knows
letters
because
stamps
told
back
house
p.20 stood
window
rain
been
was
never
longer
new
pressed
nose
against
pane
sat

45

p.21	if	**p.26**	masks		small	**p.33**	darting
	sun		Miss		which		croak
	blue		drew	**p.29**	loud		frog
	beautiful		funny		sweet		large
	rainbow		faces		masqueraders	**p.34**	cries
	went		while		gay		girls
	right		around		paint		quiet
	said		class		am		flies
	remember		child		join		tweet
p.22	clouds	**p.27**	lesson	**p.31**	morning		found
	were		so		off		call
	bumped		third		shall		grasshopper
	began		all		along		then
	cry		mouth		points		try
	cried		eyes		places		strange
	behind		laughed		factory	**p.35**	thank
	tears	**p.28**	Friday		cross		once
	different		Carnival		policeman	**p.37**	night
	colours		few	**p.32**	noise		through
	violet		costume		turns		moon
	indigo		only		follows		bright
	orange		music		narrow		light
	dried		steel		old		room
p.23	still		band		woman		round
p.24	shining		boys		leave		clock
					after		
					set		
					river		
					bridge		

	hall		
	true		
	asleep		
	seemed		
	beam		
	carried		
	float		
p.38	friendly		
	star		
	twinkled		
	used		
	sing		
	smoke		
	cow		
	dear		
	ever		
p.39	please		
	bounce		
p.40	thought		
	nodding		
	our		
	May		
	hid		
	Humpty		
	Dumpty		
p.41	jam		
	or		
	late		

The phonics programme

Vowel combinations

ai	**ea**	**oa**	**oi**	**ou**
tail	eat	boat	join	out
rain	each	road	noise	about
paint	beach	float	point	round
again	cheap	croak	coin	house

Double **ee**   Double **oo** *short and long*

oo *short*   **oo** *long*

teeth	look	zoo
tree	book	school
need	stood	food
sweet	good	moon

Vowel and consonant combinations

ay	**oy**	**ow**
say	toy	now
day	boy	how
gay	joy	down
play	Roy	brown

Vowel and consonant combinations having the same sound

er	ir	ur	or
her	shirt	nurse	word
mother	girl	turn	work
Peter	bird	burn	worm
	stir	hurt	

Special words

Words to remember

high	cry	chalk	could	laugh	because
bright	dry	talk	should	quiet	thought
light	fly	walk	would	friend	through

Say these words

| right | no | too | hear | their | knows |
| write | know | two | here | there | nose |

Look at these words

work	working	come	coming	nod	nodding
play	playing	give	giving	skip	skipping
look	looking	make	making	sit	sitting